Real Estate Confidential:

What New Agents & Aspiring Agents Need to Know

By M.J. May

Copyright Page

Copyright © 2017 by Michael John May (M.J. May)
All rights reserved. No part of this work covered by the copyright hereon may be reproduced or used in any form or by any means – graphic, electronic, or mechanical, including photocopying, recording, taping, or information storage and retrieval systems – without written permission of the author.

ISBN: 9781973134251

Disclaimer: The advice and strategies found within this book may not be suitable for every situation. This work is sold with the understanding that the author/publisher has no responsibility for the results accrued by virtue of the advice in this book.

Table of Contents

Introduction

This Is Not Easy Money

A Good Broker is EVERYTHING

Business 101: Have a Plan

May I Sell Your House?

Who Would Buy This House?

Can't Be a Secret Agent

Everyone Gets a Cut – Commissions

Always on Call...#RealtorProblems

Career Growth: Changing Your Focus

Branding: Personalities in Real Estate

Before You Go – Remember

Bibliography

Introduction

M.J. May is a licensed Louisiana real estate agent working in the New Orleans metropolitan area. He became an agent in 2015. Since then he has come to the realization that life as a real estate professional might not be the optimum career choice for him. Mr. May is not particularly disillusioned by the business, but he acknowledges that his brief tenure in this industry has been more challenging than initially imagined. According to May, there are numerous articles and forums online that give some insight into what life is like for new agents in real estate, but many of these articles and forums lack substance. This book is for new agents and aspiring agents who want to know what life is like in this industry from all aspects. May hopes this book provides you with pertinent information and enjoyment as you contemplate embarking on a career as a real estate agent.

This Is Not Easy Money

When the typical consumer thinks about the lives of real estate agents, it's difficult not to associate the concept of "easy money" with a career in real estate. Think about it, how many times have you watched one of those shows on television that depict agents showing multiple properties to clients while closing numerous deals in a time span of a mere 30 minutes to an hour? I don't even have to name these shows because you're probably thinking about at least two of them at this very moment. Don't get me wrong, I love shows about real estate. In fact, I will go on record as saying these shows helped me build up enough courage to pursue a career in real estate. But, I would be remiss if I didn't acknowledge how much these shows glamorize the industry by only showing a small portion of life as a real estate agent.

One of my favorite quotes about real estate comes from "Real Estate Jedi," Bart Vickrey. Vickrey, an agent from Valparaiso, IN, describes real estate as "a business like no other, an outsider truly has no idea what it's like, until they become an insider, and then it's too late!" There is a common misconception amongst consumers that being a real estate agent leads to easy money. Real Estate is a business, and it's not an easy one. I can assure you that every commission check that I have received in my career was earned, with extra emphasis on the word earned. If you do a Google search you will find an alarming statistic that says 87% of all agents fail in real estate in the first 5 years. As a new agent in the business, or as someone who aspires to be an agent, reading a statement such as this one can be discouraging. However, it is important to consider that new agents fail in real estate for a variety of reasons. Some agents lack the finances to maintain their business expenses over a period of time. Other agents lack the motivation to be active in the business. And then, there are those agents who are simply not meant to be real estate agents; it's just not a good career fit for their respective personalities.

Whether you think one of these groups of agents is applicable to you is not important. What is important is that you recognize how being a new real estate agent requires hard work, a particular level of focus, dedication, perseverance, and financial stability. Depending on what state you live in, the initial startup cost to become a real estate agent is approximately $1,500 - $2,000. This money typically covers fees for your pre-licensing courses, licensing exam (state & national), post-licensing courses, board dues (if your broker requires agents to be a member of the National Association of Realtors), business cards, and other marketing expenses such as signs, a customer relationship management(CRM) system, and additional advertising (if applicable). By the way, yes there is a difference between Realtors and Real Estate Agents; they are not interchangeable terms. An individual must be a member of a REALTOR® board to gain the privilege of referring to his or herself as a Realtor. Are you feeling overwhelmed yet? It's okay if you are, but don't let these initial costs and industry verbiage deter you from pursuing a career in real estate, especially if you have a passion for this business. The startup costs for a career in real estate are quite feasible in comparison to the startup costs for other businesses such as restaurants. And if you are as fortunate as me, you may be able to find a brokerage that helps alleviate some of those initial expenses. My first sales manager at my initial brokerage helped me immensely by providing a scholarship that only required me to pay $400 to take the pre-licensing courses. Furthermore, my professional headshot, business cards, access to signs, the post-licensing courses, and a free website for three months, were included in the scholarship package at no additional cost to me. The only caveat of this arrangement was that I couldn't leave the brokerage within my first year of being licensed, which is not a bad deal if you ask me. Keep in mind, that not all brokerages will provide this initial help to new and aspiring agents. Therefore, make sure you do your due diligence before deciding to hang your license with a particular brokerage.

A Good Broker is EVERYTHING

Okay, so maybe the title for this chapter sounds like something a millennial would say. But, as a millennial whose first career is being an agent in the real estate industry, I can attest to the importance of having a quality sales manager at an equally quality brokerage. Choosing the brokerage to hang your license with is undoubtedly the most important decision that you will make as a new agent or as someone who aspires to be a new agent. Agents are typically classified as independent contractors, which means you are not an employee and are responsible for managing your business in the manner that you choose. This arrangement is beneficial because you get to determine your work schedule, but as a newer agent you will probably be spending the majority of your time at the brokerage anyway. That's why choosing the correct brokerage for your needs is so vital to having success in this business. When I was starting out as a new agent I had no idea what I was doing, especially considering my lack of previous experience within real estate. I was never a homeowner, buyer, renter, investor, etc. Listing agreements, addendums, and other real estate related forms were foreign concepts to me. In many respects, it was quite overwhelming to sell property in the initial months after earning my license. Thankfully, my first brokerage offered frequent classes on a multitude of subjects that were accessible to agents at any level in their respective careers.

    Despite the numerous classes at my disposal, I quickly discovered that the only way to truly enhance your abilities as an agent is through on-the-job training. Although it can be daunting to go out into the world and secure clients when you're initially starting out, it is an imperative step if you want to evolve as an agent. A good brokerage will have systems in place to ensure your success. Brokerages need you to make money so they can make money. Be mindful of your commission split with your brokerage. Money isn't everything, but it should be an important factor in your decision of where you choose to hang your license. Some brokerages may offer great training programs, but feature less than favorable commission splits. Company culture is also a critical component to success. Every brokerage is different. I've seen brokerages that offer their agents favorable splits where the agent receives a higher percentage of the commission than the company does. However, these brokerages also had desk fees and other monthly expenses that the agent was responsible for paying. There is more information about commission splits and fees in chapter 7 of this book. Nevertheless, the culture of brokerages takes precedence. There are brokerages that feature a culture that encourages competition. Competition is not a bad thing, but it can become toxic when agents in an office feel like they are pitted against one another, leading to a sense of isolation that breeds insecurity. In this scenario, a new agent might feel at a disadvantage in comparison with agents who have years of experience.

As you begin your search for a brokerage, or if you have already decided on one, remember it's about finding the best fit for you and your business. As a new agent, or an aspiring agent, your first brokerage will go a long way in determining your success as a real estate agent. Don't be afraid to ask questions while interviewing with various brokerages. There are brokerages that will literally take anyone who has a pulse and a real estate license. These types of brokerages don't care about you or your business; they just want your money, which will be collected via the fees associated with hanging your license with the company. At this point, you have either a strong desire to become a new agent, or you're already a newly licensed agent looking for some advice. Therefore, you owe it to yourself to be incredibly thorough in the search for a brokerage. Most people will do business with you as their designated agent regardless of your brokerage affiliation because they trust you with their business affairs. But, having a reputable well known brokerage behind you certainly does not hurt your chances of growing your business. Being a real estate agent is like having a small business; you need to be thinking like a business owner at all times.

Business 101: Have a Plan

For new agents in particular, most of your daily activities will consist of establishing business via your sphere of influence. Sphere of influence is a term that you will frequently hear as a real estate agent. What is sphere of influence? In real estate, your sphere of influence consists of the people you know, including but not limited to: family, friends, acquaintances, etc. In order to build your real estate business you must avoid the trap of treating this profession as a hobby. Even if being a real estate agent is your hobby, by the way it's a very expensive hobby; you still need to implement a business plan. Now, if you thrive in organized chaos like me, then your plan can be more of an outline. Ultimately, you just need to make sure that you have some kind of strategy for achieving sustainable success.

A solid business plan or outline will help you with time management. The first phase of your business should be spent on prospecting. As a new agent you will need to cultivate a steady stream of clients if you want to have a steady stream of income. Start by reaching out to your sphere of influence. These people should be happy to hear from you; don't immediately discuss business. Instead, let the conversation gradually progress into the topic of what's new in your life. This is the opportunity for you to disclose that you are a licensed agent and are looking for clients. It is imperative that you phrase the question to members of your sphere by saying "who do you know that might be interested in buying or selling real estate in the near future?" If you were to say, "Do you know anyone...?" – More than likely the response will be "no". However, using "who" essentially encourages the other party to think more critically about their own sphere of influence. More often than not, you will get a lead by phrasing the question in this manner. The lead may be someone who is not ready to buy or sell immediately, but that shouldn't prevent you from building a rapport with the individual. Make contact with him or her and listen to their real estate needs. Add them to your CRM as well so that you can send relevant correspondence that will hopefully influence them to use you as their agent in the future.

As we discussed earlier, a good customer relationship management (CRM) system is a necessary marketing tool for all real estate agents. Every member of your sphere of influence needs to be in your CRM. As you meet other real estate professionals throughout the duration of your career, they should be added as well. Your goal is to become well-versed in all things real estate. You need to have contacts that are inspectors, appraisers, loan officers, closing attorneys, potential buyers, potential sellers, and so-on; I think you get the idea. Your business will grow as your sphere of influence grows. Who you know is just as important as what you know. Once you establish your initial contact list, the next phase is to make sure you follow up with them through timely relevant correspondence.

Following up with the contacts that you acquire is more important than the initial prospecting you do as a new agent. People can have a tendency to forget individuals if they don't interact with them on a daily basis. Moreover, I can assure you, people will forget that you're a real estate agent if you go over a year without having some type of correspondence with them. It's not atypical for members of your own family to forget that you're in real estate if they haven't heard from you since your initial announcement. Therefore, make sure to send periodic emails featuring information about your local real estate market, national news about real estate, and fun entertaining post that will encourage your audience to engage with the content. For branding purposes, in the emails you should consider adding the link(s) to your website and/or blog, which adds a personal connection to your business that may encourage readers to interact with you on a more consistent basis. As you interact with potential clients, don't forget to engage your fellow real estate colleagues as well.

It is vital for the success of your business that you consistently follow up with other agents, especially if there is a potential deal at stake. Case in point, I was selling a vacant lot and received a text from an agent who said he had a client who was interested in making an offer on the listing. The agent also told me that his client was looking at other vacant lot listings in the area so he would have to "get back with me later." After waiting two days, I decided to text the agent back to see if his client was still interested in making an offer on my listing. The agent responded by letting me know that his client was indeed still interested and we began to negotiate the terms of the purchase agreement. The moral of this story is: in this business you need to be proactive instead of reactive. If I didn't follow up with this agent, who knows what might have happened. Perhaps his client would have moved on to another property. Maybe the agent would have waited to see if my listing would become stale after a prolonged period of being on the market. While it is difficult to speculate what may have happened, my proactive actions prevented any of these hypothetical situations from becoming an actuality. Real estate agents are typically always working on multiple projects. Therefore, it's understandable if an agent forgets to follow up with you about a property. As a new agent you will encounter other colleagues who just refuse to respond and communicate with you in any capacity. Usually, these particular agents, many of whom work in the business both full-time and part-time, aren't necessarily busy, they're just inconsiderate. With the popularity of social media, there are no longer any excuses for not communicating with fellow agents, even if it's just about a simple inquiry on a particular property.

Breaking News: social media is not a fad, it's here to stay. Whether you like it or not, your real estate business will need to have an online presence in order to be relevant in today's marketplace. A good way to increase your online presence is through your social media profiles. The prevailing rule about posting content is that you should ideally have a balance between personal posts and professional business related posts. If you only post content about your business it may make your audience feel like you're nothing more than a single-minded salesperson who has an agenda. If you just post content about your personal life it may make your audience forget that you are a real estate professional who can offer them a valuable service.

Speaking from the perspective of an *unconventional* millennial, whose social media presence could best be described as nonexistent, I understand how having no social media presence severely hurts your credibility as a real estate agent. As a result, my real estate business and personal connection with others has suffered. Learn from my missteps and be consistently active on social media; it does have an impact. In addition to social media, don't forget to increase your CRM by expanding your sphere of influence through prospecting and following up with those contacts that you make. All of these tasks are essential if you desire to get to the fun part of real estate: The Houses!

May I Sell Your House?

Let's say you have your real estate license, attain a listing appointment, and successfully get the listing. Congratulations! For many new real estate agents, acquiring listings can be challenging. Some experienced agents will testify that listings are the backbone for their respective businesses. In fact, a real estate broker would frequently tell me to "get listings, always, always, always get listings, because they are easy to manage and make life as an agent less stressful." WRONG...

Here's the thing about listings, they are great to have because they provide agents with consistent business. And in many respects, working listings is a lot easier and less stressful than working with buyers, who have a tendency to vacillate in their decision making. However, new agents and those thinking about becoming agents may not be aware of the challenges that arise when you're representing the seller. Sometimes you get lucky as an agent—the seller is agreeable, the property is vacant, and the property is in good to excellent condition. Yet, more often than not, you won't be so fortunate. Every listing comes with particular variables that you as an agent must overcome. For example, what happens when you are working with multiple sellers? Maybe it's a husband and wife, or it could be the beneficiaries of a recently deceased individual. In any case, you will discover that working with multiple sellers who possess varying personalities can be not only stressful, but incredibly time consuming as well. Multiple sellers of a property can also have a tendency to disagree about a property's value, especially when a familial connection to the property is present.

Emotions are always going to be a factor in the real estate business. Sellers are typically emotional in general; these emotions are heightened when there is a sense of loss involved. For example, when children are selling the home that their parents raised them in, it can evoke an added layer of feelings that will assuredly make your job of selling the property more difficult. One child may view the property as special because of its family history and might not want to sell it immediately, while the other child may just want to sell the property quickly for the best offer that comes along. As an agent in this scenario, you will have to put on your proverbial counselor hat and try to mediate the situation before it becomes more contentious. Rule 101 of client/agent relations involves establishing expectations early at the listing appointment. Your client or clients look to you as the expert. As an agent you must be confident enough in your own abilities to successfully guide the sale of someone's home. If you're not confident, any rapport that you may have previously established with your seller will quickly deteriorate.

Lacking confidence often leads to complications for new agents, particularly when working with a seller that has an aggressive take-charge attitude. For example, some sellers may not want a sign on their property because they don't want the neighbors to know about the impending move. As an agent, particularly a newer agent, you would like to have your sign on the property for exposure purposes. But, the first priority is to make sure that your client is happy, so you can always work around not having a sign on the property. Another challenge that may befall the listing agent is the scheduling of showings. When a home is owner occupied the onus to establish a firm schedule of times to show the property is on you as the agent. Some sellers will be inflexible and demand that their home only be shown on the weekend, or only one day of the week. That's fine, but make sure to let your client know that they are potentially missing out on buyers when a rigid showing schedule is implemented. Similarly to not having a sign, a rigid showing schedule is an inconvenience to agents, but it's definitely something you can work around as well. However, the one thing that agents cannot work around, are sellers who insist on being present for all open houses and private showings. This is not only a frustrating aspect of the business, but it is also an example of the egregious disrespect that can arise between the agent and client when the agent fails to set expectations early. Buyers don't feel comfortable looking around a property when the seller is present. Furthermore, as a listing agent it makes you appear unprofessional; the seller hovering around during a showing and/or open house demonstrates the client's lack of faith and trust in your abilities to sell the property effectively. Again, to avoid these scenarios, it is in your best interest as the agent to set firm expectations during the listing appointment. When you're a new agent it can be intimidating at first, but a confident disposition and a firm belief in your abilities to market and sell properties will impress sellers and make life as a listing agent less stressful.

In case it isn't obvious, houses do not sell themselves. There are no perfect properties, not even new builds. Real Estate is a matchmaking business and as an agent you are the matchmaker. Your ultimate goal for every listing is to match that unique purchaser with the unique property that you have listed for sale. Set expectations early, but most importantly, have a plan. Establish how and where you will market the property. A good way to begin this process is by getting someone to take professional photos of the property; it will definitely help you with your digital marketing. There are certainly numerous components involved when listing a property for sale; but all of this seems simple enough, right?

Who Would Buy This House?

Believe it or not, buyers can be just as emotional and temperamental as sellers, which is understandable considering the amount of money that is typically at stake in a real estate transaction. Similarly to listing agents, agents who work with buyers will also encounter challenges. Have you ever heard the expression, "buyers are liars"? It's a real estate cliché that does have some validity in certain circumstances. Some buyers aren't always forthcoming with information. For example, there are buyers who will omit the truth about their current financial status. Some buyers may be unaware that they lack the sufficient funds to purchase property, while others are simply time wasters who want to look at homes that they know they cannot afford. An initial meeting in the office or at a public place is a good way to learn more about your buyer. Furthermore, it is incumbent upon you as an agent to ask the tough questions pertaining to how the purchase of the property will be funded. If the buyers are not using cash to fund the purchase, then you need to suggest that they speak with a loan officer to get pre-approval for a loan. The loan officer will write up a form that explicitly states how much the prospective buyer(s) can afford based on his or her respective financial situation. This helps you as the agent gain clarity on what the buyers can afford to purchase, which will make selecting properties to show an easier task.

Unfortunately, not every prospective buyer will receive pre-approval for a loan. So what are the next steps that you need to take as an agent? Will you just say you can't help them at all? No, we know being a real estate agent is all about relationships. Just because someone is not prepared to buy now doesn't mean that they will never be ready to buy. Buyers can fall into many different categories. There are four categories of buyers; the initial meeting provides you with the opportunity to identify which one of the categories best suits the prospective buyer clientele. Those buyers who have pre-approval are your potential clients. Clients need a home now. There are no outside factors preventing them from purchasing a property. The next category of buyers is comprised of prospects. Prospects want a home soon. Typically, prospects will have a set time frame for their respective impending home purchases. Prospects may or may not have outside factors influencing their home buying needs, such as a home that is currently on the market for sale. The next category features the suspects. Suspects are people who maybe want to purchase a home; the key word being maybe. These are the "lookers." Suspects want to see what's on the market, but they have no real intentions of buying a house. Finally, we have the not-yets. People in the not-yet category want a home, but can't afford one. There may be extenuating circumstances preventing members of this group from purchasing a home such as, not enough income, severe student loan debt, and/or a lack of sufficient credit. Ultimately, unless the prospective buyers appear to be unscrupulous characters, you should never dismiss any potential buyer lead. Members of the suspects and not yet categories can eventually turn into prospects and clients. The goal as a new agent is to build up your sphere of influence as much as possible. Stay in contact with all of your prospective buyers.

Consistent contact and communication can make or break the career of agents who work exclusively with buyers. As an agent you have the option of asking your buyer clients to sign an agreement that legally binds them to you as their designated agent for an agreed upon period of time. Now, I don't recommend doing this if you're representing a family member, but the agreement provides you as an agent with more protection from potentially being cut out of a deal. Remember when I said "buyers are liars" is a common expression in the real estate industry? There are instances in which a buyer's agent can get excluded from a deal, which is particularly painful if you have done a significant amount of work for the client. An example of this situation occurring usually happens when your clients visit an open house without you. The listing agent at the open house might insist that they act as a dual agent to facilitate a deal involving your buyer clients. Sometimes buyers may be unaware they are cutting their agent out of the deal. So, how can agents who represent buyers prevent losing out on a commission? Well, the buyer's agreement can prevent it, but if your buyers don't sign the agreement for whatever reason, there are other remedies to prevent your client from being poached. Most reputable agents, whether they represent sellers, buyers, or both will always ask people if they are currently working with an agent. However, in the event that they don't ask this question, make sure you provide your buyer clients with ample amounts of your business cards to hand out to other agents at open houses. As a real estate agent it is difficult to always know what your buyer clients are doing when you're not spending time with them. And time is perhaps the most important aspect in the real estate industry.

As human beings, time is our most valuable commodity. Some agents, particularly new and aspiring agents believe that they will be in charge of their own schedule. While this notion does have some validity, your schedule as an agent is primarily dictated by your clients' schedule. When your clients are off from work, you are working diligently to show them properties that fit their criteria. Understand that you will need to be flexible if you choose this career path. Money can always be earned, but we cannot recapture the time that we lose. Know your worth. Don't waste your clients' time and make sure your clients treat you in the same manner. Wasted time never results in something positive for anyone involved in a real estate transaction.

Can't Be a Secret Agent

In this business you can't be a secret agent. As a new agent in the business you will hear this expression quite often. It's yet another real estate cliché that has an element of truth. Many new agents fail to recognize how important it is for them to promote not only their respective businesses, but also themselves as well; both you and your business are a package deal. Consequently, when new agents fail to contact and/or expand their existing sphere of influence it can result in the demise of a career before it even begins. As a kid, perhaps your mother told you to never talk to strangers. Well, once you become a real estate agent that advice needs to be discarded. Don't get me wrong, I still abide by the stranger danger concept, but as a real estate agent I understand the importance of networking. Take advantage of your present sphere of influence and expand it by connecting with other people; it's the only way to grow your business.

Chances are when you initially receive your license and sign on at a brokerage, the company will provide you with an email account. Within a few days you will be inundated with emails from other agents and real estate professionals who work for a multitude of companies. These fellow real estate professionals usually purchase different real estate companies' office email lists, which is how they acquire your information. As a new agent you will probably not know who these people are, but that doesn't mean that you shouldn't add them to your CRM. Think about it, other real estate agents and professionals purchased access to your contact information, but you got theirs for free. Use these newly acquired contacts to market your listings to a wide array of real estate professionals. You never know who has that investor client looking to purchase multiple properties to enhance their real estate portfolio. And for the sake of wordplay, I'll let you in on a secret: most agents don't care how you got their information; they care about whether you can get a deal to close.

Similarly to working with the public, new agents must also become adept at working with other agents. No two agents are the same. Some agents may be tenacious negotiators, while other agents might be more accommodating by yielding to your requests. And as previously mentioned, there are those real estate agents who fail to return phone inquiries, an incredibly annoying aspect of the business to say the least. I mean seriously, we now live in a world where text messaging is the preferred method of communication. So, would it be asking too much to get a simple text back updating me on the status of a listing? But I digress; that's enough of my tangent. Essentially, be aware that as a new agent you will notice the varying personalities of other agents, particularly those who work at your brokerage.

Make a habit, or as I like to say, get into the routine of spending time at your brokerage's office either every day, or at the very least, three days a week. This is why choosing the proper brokerage is so essential for new agents. Earlier, I said a good broker is everything. Choosing the right one to hang your license with involves finding the best fit for you, and the culture of an office environment cannot be overlooked. About half of the agents in the office at my initial brokerage were older, retired, and/or just did real estate part-time. The other half were regularly active in the business, but few were willing to assist new agents like myself. Conversely, after visiting another branch office of the same brokerage, it was remarkable to see the camaraderie between the agents there, who were supportive of one another and willing to impart knowledge to their fellow agents. Regardless of what type of culture your chosen real estate brokerage's office has, there is always a learning opportunity for you as a new agent.

When you're in the office, study what the successful agents do. More importantly, study what the unsuccessful agents do, because, these agents will show you what you shouldn't be doing in the business. If possible, find and develop a relationship with an experienced agent who will mentor you. As you begin to grow your business, perhaps you can become an assistant to a veteran agent and still work your own deals on the side. The goal is to always expand. Expand your knowledge, expand your sphere of influence, and eventually, expand your income. Most of all, own the fact that you are a real estate agent. To put it simply, in this commission based industry, you can't be a secret agent.

Everyone Gets a Cut – Commissions

Ah, commissions. I'm not going to lie to you; the allure of earning thousands of dollars for selling one property is enticing. As we discussed earlier in, *A Good Broker is EVERYTHING*, as a real estate agent you will not be an employee who earns an hourly wage. You will only receive payment after successfully completing the closing of a transaction. Currently, I am aware of only one real estate company that classifies real estate agents as employees instead of independent contractors. Nevertheless, as a real estate agent who wants long-term success, if you're not closing any deals, then you will not be able to earn a livable wage.

Commissions are established by the listing agreement between the seller of a property and the listing agent of that property. Commission percentages are negotiable. Therefore, there is no standard fixed amount for commissions. Also featured in the listing agreement is the commission percentage, or the amount of money that will be shared with the cooperating broker once the listing successfully closes. The key phrase in the previous sentence is cooperating broker. Since you will be an agent and not a real estate broker who owns his or her own company, you will have to split your hard earned commission with your chosen brokerage. Legally speaking this is understandable, considering listing agreements are contracts between sellers and the brokerage; the agent is just the representative for the sellers. Thus, it makes sense for all agents, especially new agents, to negotiate a favorable commission split with their chosen brokerage. With the sheer cost of doing business, it behooves you as an agent to fight for and negotiate the best split possible, even if you are essentially brand new to the business.

Commission splits with brokerages vary. They can range from the 70/30 split, to a 50/50 split, or even a 100% commission split. Depending on your arrangement with your broker, the 70/30 split involves 70% of the proceeds from a sale going to either you as the agent or to your brokerage. The remaining 30% then belongs to the party who didn't receive the 70%. The 50/50 split is fairly self explanatory—you get half as the agent and your brokerage gets the other half. In the 100% commission split model you will earn 100% of the commissions for the deals that you close. However, in this scenario, your brokerage will take out a transaction fee per each deal closed. So, technically it's not really 100% commission, but it is certainly more money for the agent in comparison to the 70/30 and 50/50 splits respectively. It's important to note that these are simply three examples of real estate agent/broker splits that companies offer. However, depending on the brokerage, there are other types of commission splits available to agents as well. Below in more detail, are monetary examples of the different commission splits that I have mentioned. Keep in mind that the following total commission numbers do not reflect the subtraction of additional fees, such as errors and omissions insurance, which is required in certain states. Most additional fees are typically nominal.

Ex. As an agent you sell a property for $150,000 with a total commission of 6%. Unless you're acting as a dual agent, the total commission percentage is shared with the other agent and his or her brokerage, leaving you with 3% of the deal. Your split with your brokerage is? 70/30, 50/50, or 100%?

$150,000 (0.06) → 6 percent commission

= $9,000 → Total commission due from the sale of the property

70/30 Split

70% to you

30% to your brokerage

$150,000 (0.03) → 3 percent commission

= $4,500 → **Total commission due to your brokerage**

$4,500 (.70) → 70 percent to you	$4,500 (.30) → 30 percent to brokerage
= $3,150	= $1,350

50/50 Split

50% to you

50% to your brokerage

$150,000 (0.03) → 3 percent commission

= $4,500 → Total commission due to your brokerage

$4,500 (.50) → 50 percent to you	$4,500 (.50) → 50 percent to brokerage
= $ 2,250	= $2,250

100% to you

$900 Brokerage Transaction Fee

$150,000 (0.03) → 3 percent commission

= $4,500 → Total commission due to your brokerage

$4,500 - $900 → Remaining $ to you	= $3,600

Also stated in, *A Good Broker is EVERYTHING*, if you have a broker that provides you as a new agent with hands-on training, then a lower commission split might be acceptable. However, if you are a new agent with some prior experience in the real estate industry and don't need as much training, then a 100% commission structure might be more appealing and suitable to you. Keep in mind, brokerages that offer 100% commission to their agents may have a different transaction fee than the one used in the previous example. In any case, being a new agent is an adjustment with a learning curve. Ultimately, you don't want to be in a predicament where you're working an inordinate amount of hours to earn a small portion of the profits from the sale of a property. Agents must deal with a multitude of obstacles just to earn a living; bad commission splits are just one of many problems that may arise. Be sure you understand what you are signing up for before fully committing yourself to life as a real estate agent.

Always on Call...#RealtorProblems

It's 9 o'clock on a Wednesday night, and you finally begin to relax. Suddenly, your cell phone rings. You recognize the number; it's that client who never seems to be satisfied with your exceptional service. For a split second, you consider not answering the call. I mean really, this is the first moment that you've had to yourself all day. Maybe you just put the kids down for bed. Perhaps you were planning on finishing reading that chapter of the book you've been stuck on for weeks now. In any case, your phone rings for the fourth time, and you realize that you have to answer, because you're a real estate agent.

The recurring theme of setting expectations upfront with clients once again takes precedence here. As an agent, you must have the difficult conversations with clients early to ensure that you don't get taken advantaged of throughout the duration of your relationship with said client. For example, in the initial meeting with a potential client you can make it known that you are only available by phone between the hours of 9am – 6pm. This gives the potential client a clear understanding of your business hours of operation. Now, there are certain instances in which this rule may be amended, such as when a situation arises that potentially puts a transaction in jeopardy. In this scenario, since the call is pertinent for both you and your clients' business interest, it makes sense to call or answer a call beyond the designated business hours. Nevertheless, the point I'm attempting to make is that it's okay, particularly for new agents who may feel intimidated early on in their respective careers, to set boundaries with clients. Failing to set expectations early may result in an agent being on call 24 hours, 7 days a week, which is certainly not an ideal situation for anyone.

As many real estate professionals can attest to, you may end up being on call anyway because there are some clients who view agents' expectations and guidelines as mere suggestions. This is one of the *#RealtorProblems* that agents encounter. If you are active on social media, particularly Twitter, there are numerous, hilariously frustrating experiences, only real estate agents can relate to. The truth is, sometimes it's not much fun being an agent. In addition to always being on call, most agents deal with preconceived notions from the general public. Some people view real estate agents as unnecessary, money hungry middlemen, who lack a sense of ethics and competency. If you don't believe me, I dare you to do a Google search and see for yourself. Some of the comments about Realtors and real estate agents are downright brutal. There are moments in this business when it feels like nobody respects the value that you offer as a real estate agent. Real estate agents spend gas money concomitant with the majority of their time coordinating showings for clients who never send any communication to say that they will no longer be able to attend the showing. Agents will hold open houses during inclement weather, only to be greeted by a less than appreciative seller who is upset that the turnout wasn't greater.

Yes, agents deal with a lot, but the life of a real estate agent is still rewarding. The previous examples of problems that real estate agents routinely encounter are not meant to deter you from pursuing a career in this business. Any career or job that you choose will have its own distinct challenges. It is better to know and be aware of the negative aspects of a career as a real estate agent when you're first getting started so that you will not be shocked or overwhelmed should a similar situation arise in your career. Furthermore, knowing the things that could go wrong can be beneficial to you as an agent. You will be able to circumvent these challenges by being proactive instead of reactive, which will ultimately enable you, in theory, to rapidly expand your business.

Career Growth: Changing Your Focus

Throughout the book we have looked at ways to cultivate business as a new agent. But what happens if you come to the realization that being a real estate agent might not be the best career for you? Perhaps it's the uncertainty of a commissions based career. Maybe you don't enjoy particular aspects of the job, such as prospecting for new business. Regardless of your reasons, you might just decide at some point in your career that you are interested in exploring different career avenues within the real estate industry, other than being an agent or a broker.

In my experience, people typically have various reasons for leaving the life of a real estate agent behind. There are older agents who enter a semi-retirement phase of their careers where they focus primarily on sending out referrals to agents who are more active in the business. Referrals only pay out if the agent working on it closes the transaction. It's not a lot of money, typically a pre-negotiated percentage, but something is better than nothing. Some former real estate agents decide that property management is a better lifestyle fit for them. There are other agents who decide to become investors, house flippers, landlords, etc. The career choices within the real estate profession are abundant.

    During my brief career as an agent, I have met two individuals who left the real estate agent life behind for careers that are more suitable to their respective needs and personalities. One former real estate agent decided to leave behind the unpredictability for a stable desk job as a loan officer. Sure, being a loan officer might seem less exciting than being an agent who is constantly on the go, constructing multiple deals at a time. But, being a loan officer is still a career where you can provide quality service by assisting people with their home buying needs.

Also, as an added bonus, you will still be working with other agents, especially those that you have previous completed deals with in the past.

The other former agent is someone who is very dear to my heart. Like me, this person is an introvert who struggled with certain necessary tasks and aspects that come when you're a real estate agent, like consistently prospecting for new business. After being an agent for one year, this individual became an office administrator (OA) at a real estate brokerage and is one of the happiest people that I know. Much like the loan officer, the office administrator left behind the real estate agent life, but continues to work in the industry by assisting real estate agents with their transactions.

The life of a real estate agent is not particularly predictable. Being a loan officer or an office administrator for a real estate office provides stability from a financial perspective, but no career is perfect. My two examples of people who decided to no longer be real estate agents is not intended to discredit anyone who is satisfied and enjoys their career as an agent, particularly my fellow introverts. In this business you will encounter other agents with varying personalities, and it is very possible for introverts to be successful as real estate agents. Yet, there are those instances in which an individual must make a career change that coincides more with his or her professional needs and passions. Although, before you decide to make any drastic changes, make sure that you have a firm understanding of yourself.

Branding: Personalities in Real Estate

Who are you? No, I'm serious; do you know who you are? It's important that you understand and acknowledge your personality before you're sold on a career as a real estate agent. Being a real estate agent has shown me that I am without question a true introvert. I always knew that I had introverted tendencies, but I used to believe that I was more outgoing. People can be more introverted, extroverted, or a combination of the two. Extroverted individuals typically thrive and replenish their energy in social settings surrounded by others. Conversely, introverts like myself, typically need to be alone to re-energize. My personality becomes an issue for me when I must frequently engage with others for prolonged periods of time. Unfortunately, this isn't the kind of business where you can afford to disengage, not even for a minute.

As we already know, you are always on call when you work as a real estate agent. Whether you're dealing with clients, other agents, lenders, inspectors, appraisers, builders, or photographers, you will need to be adaptable enough to navigate working with multiple people who possess varying personalities. So, how do you accomplish this you ask? The answer is to be your authentic self. Sometimes you may have to be a bit of an actor and play a different version of yourself, while still maintaining the true traits that make you unique. My second sales manager, a self proclaimed introvert, once told me that it's okay to have a "personal/private version of yourself and a business/professional version of yourself." If you decide to take this particular advice, the key thing to remember is consistency. People can tell when you are being disingenuous and may become reluctant to do business with you.

Your personality is your brand. Yes I know the word "brand" has become an overused buzzword perpetuated by countless celebrities through multiple social media platforms. But, as a real estate agent, your brand, more specifically, what you're known for and how you market yourself, will set you apart in a profession that quite frankly, is over-saturated. Consumers will want to work with you and trust you to handle their business only if they feel a genuine connection to you. At this point we understand the value of constant contact and communication between a real estate agent and the consumer, but there are many other considerations to think about before you commit to this career.

Earlier in *Can't Be a Secret Agent*, I said, "you and your business are a package deal." Well, have you thought about how you want the public to perceive you? Previously we examined how to use the company email to our advantage, but don't rely too heavily on that email. Create your own unique professional real estate email account. Mine is mjmayrealestate@gmail.com. By the way, feel free to drop me a line. Your email could be blanksellshouses@whatever.com; don't forget to insert your name in the "blank" placeholder. A creative personally managed professional email account is not only good for branding purposes, but it also protects you in the event that you change brokerages. When I left my original brokerage all of my contacts and emails were no longer accessible because the company was the administrator of the email account. Thankfully, I planned ahead and transferred what I needed before officially relinquishing my affiliation with this company. Yet, there are many new agents and even a few experienced agents who don't think about the consequences that arise when they don't take the time to brand themselves outside of their respective brokerages. Even if you are truly the local expert in your town, a lack of branding will essentially render you irrelevant as a real estate agent, particularly in this era, where everyone is accessing the internet for research purposes.

We already mentioned the importance of a social media presence in an earlier portion of the book. But, technology in general has become such a vital business component for several real estate agents. Many contracts are written and signed online; the days of paper are fading fast, especially once more Millennials begin to infiltrate the housing market. You don't want to become the real estate agent who is behind on the ever changing technological advances. Even if you don't use technology to service every client, I can almost guarantee you that at some point in your career you will need to not only understand technology, but also use it effectively to maintain and enhance your current client base. If you're reluctant to engage with others through social media or have a tepid response to technology in general, then you should NOT under any circumstances be a real estate agent.

This is a career, not a job. It will require a level of commitment that some people may be unprepared to handle. There will be bad days that will make you want to quit, especially in the beginning of your career. But, if you persevere, there will be triumphant days as well. Much like life, in real estate there are no guarantees. So whether or not you decide to pursue a career in this industry, I hope this book was an educational resource that provided you with a satisfying informative experience.

Before You Go – Remember

- A career as a real estate agent does **NOT** equal easy money.
- Many new real estate agents fail for a variety of reasons.
- The initial startup cost to become a real estate agent varies, but it is not as expensive as some other business ventures.
- If possible, try to find a brokerage that offers some assistance with your initial startup cost.
- **Interview with as many different brokerages as you can.** Choosing a brokerage to hang your license with is an important decision & should not be taken lightly.
- **Every commission check will be earned**, with extra emphasis on the word, **earned**.

- As a new agent **you must prospect to build upon your current sphere of influence**.
- You will need some kind of strategy for success – **Implement a business plan or at the very least, a business outline.**
- Steady stream of clients = Steady stream of income
- Make contacts with people who work in all facets of the real estate profession and add them to your customer relationship management (CRM) system.
- You will **absolutely** need some kind of online presence: social media, blog, company website.
- As a real estate agent you need to **be proactive instead of reactive**.

- Listings provide consistent business, but can require a lot of work, particularly when multiple sellers are involved in a transaction.
- Don't be afraid to ask your clients the tough questions (i.e. Finances).
- **Always build relationships** – Even if a potential client isn't currently ready to do business, send them relevant correspondence via your CRM.
- Although you're a new agent, **keep a confident disposition**. Failing to do so could cost you business.
- This is an emotional business. You will need to adapt accordingly.
- **Set firm expectations with clients early at the initial meeting.**

- The initial meeting with any new prospective clients should **always** take place in a public setting (preferably at the office).
- **Time is a valuable commodity.** Don't waste your time or your clients' time and request that your clients treat you in the same manner.
- You can't be a secret agent.
- You must promote not only your business, but also yourself as well.
- **Give your business cards out to everyone that you meet.**
- Failing to grow your sphere of influence will end your career before it begins.
- As a real estate agent **you will most likely be classified as an independent contractor for tax purposes. Make sure you understand what that means.**

- Brokerages offer different commission splits to agents. Find the best fit for you and your business.
- As a real estate agent, you will be on call.
- Know that if you choose this career path, the public will undervalue what you have to offer.
- Despite the challenges, **being a real estate agent is a rewarding career.**
- If you have a difficult day and need a laugh – Search #RealtorProblems on Twitter.
- **Embrace technology. Brand yourself outside of your chosen real estate company** by creating a unique professional email account that you personally manage.
- Real estate agents come in all sizes, shapes, and personality traits. Don't think you have to be a certain way in order to be successful.

- It's okay if you come to the realization that you don't enjoy being a real estate agent. This business is not for everyone.

Most of All…

- Know who you are – never change to placate anyone.

Thanks for Reading

Bibliography

Online Resources

Google Search: "real estate agents fail"

Ferry, Tom. "87% of All Agents Fail in Real Estate" http://www.tomferry.com/blog/87-of-all-agents-fail-in-real-estate/
*Note: Statistic is from a 2014 report by the National Association of Realtors (NAR)

Vickrey, Bart. *The Good Life Newsletter*. "Talking Yourself Off the Ledge." 19 June 2017.

www.ingramcontent.com/pod-product-compliance
Lightning Source LLC
Chambersburg PA
CBHW031542210526
45464CB00003B/1117